STRONG MOMS

COMPILED BY SHEILA WEBSTER
RUTH L. SNYDER

Copyright © 2023 by Compiled by Sheila Webster & Ruth L. Snyder

All rights reserved.

No part of this book may be reproduced in any form or by any electronic or mechanical means, including information storage and retrieval systems, without written permission from the author, except for the use of brief quotations in a book review.

Paperback: 978-1-7771313-6-4

Ebook: 978-1-7771313-5-7

DEDICATION

This book is dedicated to our good friend, Bobbi Junior. She was a fellow writer and a strong mother.

Her first daughter only lived a couple days and the story was chronicled in her book "When the Bough Breaks."

When her next daughter was just fifteen, she became a quadriplegic and Bobbi rose to the occasion of learning to care for her. During this time Bobbi's mom started down the road of dementia. (This story is told in Bobbi's award-winning book, "The Reluctant Caregiver.")

Bobbi had a severe hearing loss, but was always encouraging, helpful, and positive.

She passed away on December 2020 while awaiting a lifesaving liver transplant.

Thanks, Bobbi, for your inspiration

CONTENTS

1. Becoming A Mom   1
2. The Perfect Plan   9
3. Choices   23
4. New Challenges   29
5. My "Another Mother"   41
6. A Military Take Over   49
7. I am Strong   55
8. On Losing A Child   63
9. These Moments of Motherhood   69
10. Does Her Heart Break Like Mine?   73
11. The Strengths of My Mother   91

1

BECOMING A MOM

BY RUTH L. SNYDER

*E*ver since I can remember I wanted to be a mom. My plan was simple. First, I would get married. Then I would get pregnant and give birth to many children and of course be a happy mom. However, as you know, plans don't always work the way we think they will.

I was 25 when I married Kendall. After a couple of years of trying to get pregnant, we went to see a fertility specialist. He told us that barring a miracle, we would never have children of our own. However, a few months later, to my great joy and astonishment, I discovered I was pregnant. A few short weeks after that, I had a miscarriage and plunged into despair and anger. I grieved deeply. No matter how hard we tried, another pregnancy did not become a reality.

I felt like I was stuck in no man's land. Hearing about others who became pregnant without trying and then didn't take care of their children made me angry. Why were my arms empty while theirs were full? Mother's Day was painful. My husband told me the day wasn't for me because I wasn't a mother yet.

We started discussing adoption. Kendall was hesitant, so we waited another year or so. The night that we sat down to fill out adoption application forms, the phone rang. Our sister-in-law was calling us to ask if we would consider adopting her niece, an 8-month-old baby. She gave us the relevant information and asked us to get back to her as soon as possible. We decided to proceed, even though Sue told us we should be ready to pick up our new daughter the following Monday. We had four whole days to get ready to become parents.

The three-hour drive to Mary's house seemed to take forever. Sue met us there to be a support for her sister. We walked into the mobile trailer and Mary had all the belongings for her baby beside the door ready to go. I will always remember the mixed feelings I experienced as Mary placed baby Paige in my arms. Joy for the gift I received intermingled with sorrow and respect for the difficult choice Mary made. Mary also handed me a handwritten letter to give to Paige when she was older. In the letter, Mary explained she wasn't giving up her baby because she didn't want her. She was placing her baby in our home because she wanted Paige to grow up in a home with two parents. She wanted the very best for her baby.

I had taken care of many babies as a babysitter. But I soon discovered having an infant in my care 24/7 was more complicated than I thought it would be. What did infants eat? How often? How could I soothe my new daughter when I had already fed her and changed her diaper and she was still crying? What was Paige used to? We learned by trial and error, just like most parents do.

When we picked Paige up, Mary had signed a document for relative adoption. However, when we consulted a lawyer, he informed us we didn't qualify as relatives because we were not related to Paige by blood. The lawyer stressed that if Mary changed her mind at any time, the law required us to give Paige back. He also told us not to contact Mary directly, as that could hinder the adoption process down the road. Instead, Sue was to have all contact with her sister, including asking Mary to go to the Welfare office to sign the correct documents.

Six long months later, Sue informed us that Mary's father committed suicide. We thought for sure she would want her baby back. However, a couple days later, Sue said that Mary told her this unforeseen death had convinced her Paige needed a healthy home. She signed the papers relinquishing her parenting rights and consenting to us adopting her baby. However, Mary still had twenty-one days to reconsider her choice. Those 21 days seemed to drag by. I felt like I was holding my breath, waiting for something to go wrong. I jumped every time the phone rang. But Mary stayed strong. The deadline came and went. We could now proceed with our application for adoption.

The private adoption process in Alberta is rigorous. First, we went to parent training. These sessions gave us more insight into the reasons children become available for adoption, difficult choices that birth parents make, the reasons behind the laws in Alberta, and all the legal formalities we needed to complete before a judge granted the adoption order. The next big hurdle was having a home study completed. The home study interview felt more like an interrogation. A social worker asked about our family history, our growing up years, our dreams, our goals, and how we would raise our child (including thoughts on discipline). Then the social worker inspected our home for safety. Finally, we completed a mountain of paperwork and sent it away to the adoption agency that was acting on our behalf. Our social worker at the adoption agency reminded us that the court process could take six months to a year.

Finally, we received notification of the court date where we would go before a judge, and they would decide whether we could adopt our daughter or not based on the adoption application. We also received a bill from the adoption agency. (Private adoptions typically cost anywhere from $5,000 to $10,oo0.)

We walked into the court room with several other families who had also applied for an adoption order. The clerk instructed us to stand while the judge entered. The judge sat down and greeted us all with a smile. He told us these adoption hearings were the best part of his job. Then he explained how the hearings would proceed and even invited us to document the finalization of our child's adoption with a photograph. Tears dripped down my face as I heard the judge grant the adoption order, legally making me a mom.

2

THE PERFECT PLAN

BY JEWELL VANSTONE

As a little girl I always played with dolls setting them up as my family, feeding them, dressing them, lining them up in a row. Having a large family was a major part of how I envisioned my life one day combined with being a nurse, country living, and owning horses. God wants to give us the desires of our heart but before I would see my story become reality made perfect by God, I would suffer greatly by my own hand.

Staring down at the tiny human I was holding in my arms so many thoughts swirled in my mind that I was unaware of anything else around me. She was the epitome of perfection in a soft pink outfit and wrapped in a light blanket. Her fine ebony hair lay close to her head and framed her sweet face with a heart-shaped mouth and pixie nose. Less than an hour ago I was still in the hospital with her after giving birth. Now the moment I had not allowed myself to imagine was upon me and I was sick at the thought of it. This child, this baby girl would soon be in someone else's arms leaving mine empty, with questions and a deep lonely ache in its place. This plan had been put in place months ago with Mark and Rose who were on their way now to complete it. Beside me lay a small envelope containing a letter—a letter I had written to her for the future in the hope that one day her parents would choose a time when it would benefit her to read it. With it I included a note to them as well giving them freedom to read it for their knowledge and approval. In my deep thoughts I had forgotten the other person in the silence with me as I awaited the inevitable. My mother sat with me, speechless, as no words could make this any more bearable and she never did express her sadness on that day or any other.

That God wants to give us the desires of our hearts has always been at the core of my faith when I pray. During high school I fell into a lifestyle of disobedience to God and this put a huge rift in my relationship with Him. Previously where such intimacy had been there was avoidance and silence. We can have no secrets from God but when I found myself locked in this pattern of behaviour I tried to convince myself that this was what I wanted and that it was my right to choose. And indeed God has given us freedom of choice but choosing against His will will always bring sorrow and regret.

Following high school graduation I went directly into nursing college as had been my lifelong goal. I had ensured that all the prerequisites were met in my credits and I was filled with nervous confidence, sure this was where I should be and my life would continue to progress exactly as I envisioned. I enrolled in the closest college of nursing to avail myself of living with my beloved 69-year-old German descent, Russian immigrant grandmother. Grandma had been widowed for two years and was happy at the thought of my company. Her location was good for me and since I had planned to make a clean break from my lifestyle and start over I planned to go to her church with her and make new friends. This was a good plan and it wasn't long before I had a social network with the College and Career group enjoying the weekly events and activities scheduled by the church planners. Grandma didn't mind when my friends came over to hang out and with that was the inevitable couple development. I soon had a boyfriend and by Christmas we were an item. School work and dating filled most of my evening hours and the months flew by. At some point the relationship ended. Looking for other places to fill my social needs I considered the invitations from casual friends at school. It wasn't long before my old habits revealed themselves in excessive drinking, partying and repeat. Friends from church took second place and when school ended for the year the same pattern followed as I moved home for the summer to my summer job. It was a rocky time with the struggle between my new found independence and living under my parents roof again which mirrored my internal struggle between God's will and my own.

The summer was a series of heated arguments between my father and myself leaving lingering hostility in the household. My bitterness grew and by the time I was due to return to school I was secretly smouldering and threatening to burst into flames at any moment.

Finally one night after a particularly scathing lashing of words I stormed off in a rage. In my wounded spirit the hurtful words spoken to me replayed over and over. Angrily I packed a bag and created a plan to disappear for a few days until I had blown off steam. I knew a guy driving a semi from Alberta to Regina so I bought a bus ticket to meet him and jumped in the truck with him to travel for the weekend partying along the way. With my former commitment to change I had stopped taking birth control and in my frenzy of alcohol and anger I allowed myself to be intimate with my friend. That error changed my life and a few weeks later I realized that I was pregnant.

I had already started my first semester of second year nursing and had no idea what to do. In fear I shared my situation with two close friends from the college and career group I had been attending and in God's perfect plan He provided a way for me. My friend's sister was in the same situation that I found myself and she had been connected with a christian minister who had handled several private adoptions for other girls like ourselves. After talking it through for hours I knew that I wanted to give this baby a life with two parents and not the life of a single parent unprepared as I was to be a parent. I prayed about it and asked God to make something good come out of this. Using this Christian man to handle the adoption would allow me to ensure that my baby went to a Christian couple and this was the most important item on my list of criteria. The thought of giving up my first child when my dream to be a mother had always been so real was excruciating but still I knew it was what I wanted to do. Making that decision was so very hard and harder still was the haunting knowledge that there would be an even harder day to come after the baby's birth. These thoughts I buried deep within my heart.

My friend helped me to contact this minister and his wife and arrange a meeting for us to discuss the details. I had not even told my parents of my situation but I felt it was crucial to make these arrangements on my own before I did that so they would know I was taking the responsibility upon myself. The plan was formed that I would finish my first semester before moving to Winnipeg where I would deliver and the adoption would be arranged in that province to protect the privacy for all involved. It seemed to fall into place so smoothly and I was sure God was in control. A christian couple was quickly found who were waiting to adopt and now it was a matter of time, patiently awaiting the day of arrival.

Through the course of the winter I made one trip home and saw several close friends who knew my situation. It was only when I got back to my temporary home in the next province I realized that everything had changed. I couldn't understand why I had such a longing to go back when originally I wanted the separation for my privacy and I found myself increasingly uneasy and restless. What I didn't know was how my decision to change provinces would complicate everything for the kind and gracious couple who had made all the arrangements for the adoption in that province. When I told them how I was feeling they were so gentle and patient with me. Never did they pressure me to stay nor did they ever tell me how this would affect them. It was only after I went home that I realized how everything had changed. I made my own arrangements and made my next temporary home in the home of my friend's parents. This was the same friend who offered the contact information for the private adoption after his sister had been in the same situation. This little family were unbelievably loving and welcoming to me and their simple home life made me comfortable instantly. What I did not know made this time truly peaceful and content for me.

Meanwhile Roger was praying for God's will to be done as he searched via his contacts for a new adoptive family. What I did not know was that by moving to another province I had caused the family in my neighboring province to be ineligible for this adoption. It was required by law to be handled within the same province where the baby was born. God's plan is perfect and he had it all under control but during the navigation of the rapids there would be some white knuckles. From my vantage point however, ignorance was bliss. I had few visitors in those last days with the main one being my closest confidant, a girl who I had connected with from nursing school and attending College and Careers together. I had trusted her with my secret and she would be my labor coach. We talked daily and one day she brought greetings from a male friend who was feeling such empathy for me that he offered to marry me so I wouldn't have to choose adoption. I know his suggestion was motivated by love, but I was committed to my decision and had no intention of changing the plan even though it was comforting to know how deeply he cared for me. The day arrived as we knew it would when I went into labor and this season of life would soon be over. My heart was a kaleidoscope of emotions and I could not begin to separate them or describe them. Many women make a decision when they choose adoption that they will not see their baby after birth, but I always felt like that was not going to work for me. I needed reality, a tangible memory to hold in my heart, to bond with my baby for those first days before she would leave my life forever. That was the thought process that drove my decision to hold my new baby girl, to memorize her face, her hairline, her nose and lips. That was why I chose to nurse her for 3 days before we were discharged from the hospital and experience the uncomfortable pressure in my breasts when she stopped to remind me of her presence in my life. Anyone who has carried a baby inside her for nine months understands the feeling of absence within her following a birth. However holding the newborn in your arms replaces that feeling and you still have the connection so many hours of the day. In my case I would be left with empty arms and a lonely heart but the memory of what it felt like to hold her in my arms and to study her face as she slept would stay with me during those sad times. Through the nights I remembered her face when I sat at the edge of my bed and wept, remembering her movement within my body.

It was years before I had another baby of my own to hold and fill that void. I would finish my Nurses Training and graduate as a Registered Nurse. I would marry, be a widow, and marry again to a farmer, live on a farm, own horses and have more children. I was content, comfortably settled in my life to that point. At a Bible School reunion involving my husband's family, my husband introduced me to a woman who used to live across the street from his family. She asked if she could speak with me privately and we moved over to the foyer together. I was puzzled by her request but I had no reason to fear or worry so I calmly waited for her to begin what she had to say. She was trembling from the top of her head to her toes as she tremulously spoke. Her voice quivered and softly she said, "I am the mother of your birth child". She took my hand in hers and examined it saying it was just like "hers". I was staring blankly at her with the same expression frozen on my face since she spoke the words. She started to give details of the day my daughter was given to her through the private adoption. She told me of how, with two little boys at home, God had spoken to her in the hospital after her third failed pregnancy and how He promised her that He would provide another baby for her. And how they had received a phone call out of the blue from Roger asking if they were thinking of adopting a baby since he had been given their names as prospective parents in the adoption he was working on. She reminded me that she had lived across the street from my husband's parents and described the scene when they arrived home with their precious bundle and the neighbor lady across the street, now my mother-in-law, rushed right over to pray a blessing over the new baby.

She had struggled to make a decision about searching for me as she had a few clues about my life and who I had married. She told God that if she could locate me at the reunion among thousands of people, she would take it as a sign that it was time for the two of us to meet. We did meet and had time to talk alone and even introduced my three younger children as well. What a gift from God that I should have the joy to meet this girl I'd given birth to before she was an adult, as I always imagined would be the case (if in fact she chose to ever meet me at all.) I have been truly blessed and have no doubt that God's plan is always perfect, it is the best for us in every way if we are patient and wait for His perfect timing.

3

CHOICES

BY GRACE LAVOIE

When I was 18, fresh out of high school and wanting my independence, I started dating someone. I thought I loved him, so I moved in with him, in his parents' basement. I had no job and was in a very toxic relationship. Through the course of 9ish months, he had cheated on me (with multiple different girls) the entire time we were together. One night I wanted to go to a party to let loose a little and have some fun. I was alone and hurting and decided to try some cocaine that a few of my "friends" had with them just for fun. Instantly I felt amazing. I forgot how much I was hurting and how messed up I made my life. I continued using pretty much only with friends or at parties. My now ex had gotten mad at me a few weeks later for I still don't know what and decided to kick me out late at night. I had nowhere to go. I texted my best friend at the time. She offered to come pick me up and I stayed with her that first night so I could have the next day to figure something out. A mutual friend of mine just had his roommate move out and had an extra room. He said I could crash there for as long as I needed.

After a few months, we started dating and my drug use continued. However, now my habit was getting so bad I was sneaking out to go buy cocaine and sitting in my car using all by myself. Instead of using during nights out I used all day and all night just to cope with how very depressed and anxious I was all the time. I was also using during all my nights out because it was "fun" and "cool". This was my rock bottom —such darkness, and it seemed like the light at the end of the tunnel was getting dimmer by the day. It really is crazy what drugs do to you, to your mind and even your body. They suppress your hunger, so I started rapidly losing weight and I was already a slim petite girl. It makes you feel invincible, like nothing will hurt you.

I didn't realize how bad things had gotten until early one morning my boyfriend found me lying in the middle of a busy highway staring up at the stars. In my drugged state, no danger at all crossed my mind even for a second. My drug use was starting to hinder our relationship and he gave me an ultimatum—I needed to quit or he would leave me. I knew he loved me and cared a lot about me, and I knew I couldn't wreck the one good thing I had in my life, so I stopped using cold turkey. With his support and my determination to be more than what I currently was, I got a job and after a few months I decided to quit smoking too.

About a week after I quit smoking, I found out I was pregnant with my first born. You see teen pregnancy all over and you never think it will happen to you until it does. I was terrified and incredibly scared to tell my parents. Growing up my parents didn't encourage me to have boyfriends and we were taught in church to save ourselves for marriage. I was scared—not so much about my parents being mad, but that they would be disappointed in me. I hated having anyone disappointed in me, still do. My now husband had bought a ring quite a while back. He said from the first time he saw me he always knew he was going to marry me. He took me for a walk around Jesse Lake here in Bonnyville and proposed to me, promising the rest of our lives together. I did get a small bit of pushback from some family members about the "proper way" of doing things and the order it should have been done but what's done is done and our only option was to push forward.

When I was younger I was very conflicted with the fact I was adopted and struggled with not feeling wanted or even questioning who "Mom" was. Now I am very grateful for both my parents, but mom especially, for always trying to understand me and showing me over the years that she has and will always be there for me. I decided to ask her to be there when our son was born, and she agreed. I want to say it was magical, but it really wasn't. After three days of labouring and 20ish minutes of pushing, childbirth sucks, but I am glad she was able to be there.

My husband and I got married the following July and had our little seven month old as our ring bearer. That's when I knew I had made it. I was with the love of my life and our gorgeous baby boy. I knew no amount of temptation would ever make me go back to where I had been. It hasn't been easy; still isn't after six years of being clean. I still think about my past and how different my life would be right now or if I would even be here if I hadn't quit. Those who want to quit using need to want to get clean themselves. No amount of others' opinions is going to change anything. My husband is my rock, and I would not be who I am today without him. Five years of marriage and two beautiful children later, we've experienced a few surgeries together, some ups and downs but we haven't been as happy as we are right now. I'm grateful that he's never given up on me no matter how stubborn I can be and that he's loved me for exactly who I am. My story has a happy ending and I will forever be thankful for that.

4

NEW CHALLENGES

BY JEWELL VANSTONE

Coming home from work I found my husband Tim frantically pacing through the house. Our seventeen-year-old daughter's luggage was packed and lining the hallway outside her room. As she packed things from her room into containers, Tim accosted me with glazed eyes, his face pale and his body rigid and voice shrill with panic. "When were you going to tell me about this?" he asked accusingly. My stomach lurched and quickly sank to my toes while my heart came up into my throat. The whole sensation made me feel like I may faint. I believe

I was speechless for several seconds before I spoke. I was shaking as I explained that in my opinion, I had already told Amy that she was not going anywhere until she had worked somewhere and saved some money. I felt the discussion was closed and that there was nothing to tell. I began to break into a cold sweat and a pain began to develop somewhere in my chest.

Nothing can really prepare you for your children to become adolescents. Watching them grow from a newborn to a toddler in what seems to be a time warp, we embrace and encourage each achievement with excitement because this is what we expect and look forward to even before birth. Tears fall when they start preschool and when they go off to kindergarten.

The independence of our children is both a source of pride and fear for a parent. Accomplishment of new challenges and growth of stature and mind gives us pleasure. They begin to express determination to make decisions and suddenly we see the possibility that they may not need us as much as they did, and we tighten our grip ever so slightly hoping to maintain control. What if they stumble, what if they fall? Soon the distance from high school graduation is much less than from the day they were born, and they consider themselves almost adults. Time evaporates through fourteen years of life when a parent was the most important supporter and advocate.

Amy Elizabeth Vanstone was born on 22 November 1986. A unique personality and her own independent nature began to reveal itself. With strong ideas of fashion, art and food, she did not accept advice or assistance easily and did not share her feelings often. Gentle yet bossy with her siblings and even friends at times, we often joked about the book "Little Miss Bossy" having a resemblance to her. Two more babies followed Amy and she developed a strong nurturing instinct towards them, treating them as a little mother hen. Silky blond locks grew to her waist by the start of kindergarten and it was a statement look for many years through grade school and into grade nine.

Our first personal computer was purchased in the late ninety's and we enjoyed all the technological advances a SASKTEL dial up internet connection could offer. This was a new age with so much fear and uncertainty of the unknown. Schools taught computer skills but we as parents had very little knowledge and heard stories which only compounded our anxiety. The internet provided MSN and teenagers everywhere talked to each other through that program rather than talking on the phone. Of course, with dial up connections like we had, the phone line was still always busy, and it was just as annoying as children talking endlessly on the telephone. But what it offered that the telephone did not was the ability to connect with people who they had never met in real time rather than with letters and conversations where you could not see or hear the person. Through MSN Amy became involved in a few chat rooms talking to people with similar interests.

She had always been a home body and never really boy crazy like some of her friends. Involvement in the local figure skating club during the winter and soft ball for a few years when she was younger gave time out of the home but other than that had no serious interest in sports. She had a few special girlfriends whom she enjoyed spending time with, but MSN offered conversation and interaction without even having to leave the house. This is where my story begins.

Upon discovering that she had been talking to a person in a chat room we were concerned and grew even more so when we found the friend was supposedly a sixteen-year-old boy from Texas. Tim became almost hysterical over the situation with all the stories we had heard telling of young people who had been lured away by online relationships and even threatened to pull the plug on the computer if she didn't stop talking to this person. I stepped in because it seemed to me that since we all made use of the computer that it was unfair to punish us all by losing use of the computer. Looking back, it may have made a difference, but we all know about hindsight.

Contact did continue with this young man whose name we discovered was William Lane. We still were not confident this was his real identity and for all we knew he could be a 40-year-old predator. Soon online communication was enhanced by web cameras and Amy got a tiny camera that was a prize for selling magazines at school. Now she could have web cam visits with this William and they spent time together every evening. When I would go down to the computer desk to monitor the situation, she became defensive and secretive. Will – as she now referred to him – would look down, away from the camera and refuse to speak until I left. This was disturbing to me but the whole scene seemed out of our control and we just didn't know what steps to take. By the time Amy was in Grade

Twelve she started to get daily phone calls from Will.

By now I had accepted that he was who he claimed as the phone calls came on our house phone from his personal cell phone. I would sometimes answer, and the call would disconnect. I spoke to Amy about it and explained that if this young man was going to be talking to our daughter, I would need to be able to talk to him as well. I asked that when he called that he would speak to me first when I answered his call. And thus, began my introduction to William Lane of Houston, Texas.

Talking to a Texan from a cell phone in 2002 was not always the clearest connection. Understanding a southern drawl over an unclear phone call was even more difficult. As I spent time talking to this Texas-born boy, I learned about his time spent in school, where he had lived, where he had worked so far and a little bit about his family. Will was a fast talker for a Texan, and I had quite a time trying to make out everything he said but I came to look forward to these conversations. A costly birthday gift of perfume arrived in the mail for Amy's seventeenth birthday. When her graduation arrived, she had already been accepted to a photography college in Saskatoon and she would be starting just a few weeks into July. She had arranged to live in a basement suite with friends in the city. Her course was only a few months and then she would be back at home looking for a job. Close to the end of her classes she informed us that she would be having a visitor that she would like to bring out to the farm for a visit.

Will was coming to Canada to see her. He wanted to meet her face to face and decide if their relationship had a future. This was a huge surprise to us and once we met him, I had such relief as we watched him interact with our family, laughing and joking and telling stories. After that one visit I thought I had a pretty good idea where this would lead, and I thought I was okay with it. But I was wrong.

While I always tried to keep the lines of communication open with all our children one never knows what they are holding within themselves. Amy did not easily share her deepest thoughts and feelings and she was thinking and planning her future with Will and waiting patiently for an opportunity. She asked for permission to use some of her graduation gift money to travel to Houston to meet Will's family which we granted without concern. She spent three weeks there with them and came home so happy.

Amy was unsuccessful in finding a job and then one evening while we were at a farewell party for a classmate of hers, she told me that Levi's dad was agreeable to take her with them to Texas. Levi was going to work there with a youth rodeo outreach program, and they were driving because Levi needed a horse for the summer. This was Monday evening and they were leaving Wednesday morning. I very strongly told her that that she could not go until she had worked and saved some money. Nothing more was said that night. I wish now that I had spoken to Levi's dad to let him know our stand on the matter. But once again hindsight is a much better viewpoint.

Now here we were on Tuesday evening with Amy packing her bags and set on leaving for Texas in the morning. Neither Tim nor I slept much that night even though we had come to a decision to take Amy to meet her friends in town. We did not see a way out of this dilemma. Amy was determined to leave with these people no matter how we felt about it and we wanted her to know we loved her unconditionally. It was a silent ride to Milestone in the early morning light of May 25, 2005. The truck and trailer were parked by the Co-op gas station when we pulled up and I hesitated to make eye contact with them as we loaded Amy's belongings. I wept as the taillights disappeared down the highway.

As the days passed by, I felt quite certain that I would die before I saw my daughter again. I talked to Will on the phone before she got there and cried to him asking him how he would feel if it was his little sister and begged him to send her home. And I cried. I cried at work, when I drove, on the phone, and while I lay in my bed. I cried endlessly when I talked to Amy on the phone and finally, told myself that if I didn't get a grip on myself my daughter would just quit calling home. So, I loved her, and reminded her of that over and over.

We talked as often as she called and I held my tears to myself. She married Will the day after her eighteenth birthday in the office of their pastor with no family present. Her explanation was that she did not want it to be complicated or costly for either family or that she had never cared about a wedding anyway.

Life eventually settled into a sort of normal with a missing piece and it was three years before we saw her face to face again. I did not die, and she came home for her brother's graduation. Will flew in close to graduation and I had all my children together in one place for two days. We thanked God for that time together. It was such a blessing to see our daughter with her husband and feel like we knew him a tiny bit better. We have never doubted that he loves our daughter and that she loves him. We pray for all our children daily and they know and take comfort in the knowledge.

"His eye is on the sparrow, and I know He is watching [me]."

5

MY "ANOTHER MOTHER"

BY JOSHUA HEATH

In my first poetry book, *Shopping Cart Boy*, I wrote a poem about my biological mother dying. She was strong in many ways, but too often in the wrong ways.

She was very strong-willed about doing her own thing, but not about getting me back from foster care. It is hard to understand even though I am a man now. Even her addictions counsellor did not realize how much she lied about what she did.

My biological mom loved me deeply. I know that. But her love wasn't the kind that could overcome hard things like her addiction. My '***another mother***' who I also wrote a poem about tells me that addictions are harder than I understand.

I am beginning to understand that too as I have been addicted to meth in my young life and if it wasn't for the love of my '*another mother*' I could not have walked away from it twice.

My mom – the one I call '*another mother*' is very strong even though she feels weak and sometimes cries a lot when hard things happen. But I would swear she gets stronger after she cries.

She is strong because she helps people, even people who have been mean to her or cursed at her or cursed her. My biological mom was very mean to her; I witnessed it sometimes with my own eyes.

She has a strong faith in everything she does and is an example in that way. She loves to teach people and her kids, skills to survive, thrive, or just for fun.

My mom visited me in jail, she was always at court and the lawyers with me. She took me off the streets and helped me get off meth twice.

My mom got me out of foster care and helped my biological mom get me back, then she helped my brother get custody of me after my biological mom died. When my brother could no longer care for me – even though she knew I would make her life hard – she took me and became my guardian.

My mom has been there for me when I run up bills, steal her stuff, lie to her, and when I am good too. She takes me on vacations and shows me how to live differently,

She helps me sell and speak about my books, and my life. She knows I don't understand a lot of things and she works very hard to teach me what things mean. She has helped me to read better, to shop, to go without and not steal.

She helps me get through hard days; when I just want to die.

. . .

ANOTHER MOTHER

No one knows

The relief

To have another mother

A real one

Who loves me

And lets me cry

And cry and cry

Till my tears stop on their own.

That teaches me things

And loves me

She listens to the bad stuff

That happened to me

And that I have done

Even when people say

STRONG MOMS

Mean things

About me being her son

She stays She smiles She is my mom.

I turn white when I am sick

She turns brown in the summer

People don't talk to her anymore

Because I am her son

But she said she prefers reality

To make believe

My favourite times

Are when we drive

Alone for miles

We look at the prairie sky

And watch the wind

On the trees and water.

We point out the deer

And eagles some moose

Coyotes or foxes

We say nothing

For hours

And get home

Late at night

we smile, we sigh and say

"That was a good drive"

She doesn't have money

For things that she would

Like sometimes for me to do

But we share tea or coffee

In pottery mugs or paper cups

And don't mind sharing

Because it makes us

STRONG MOMS

Strong family

We may not be blood

But we are hearts together

And minds made up to be

A different kind of family.

6

A MILITARY TAKE OVER

BY JEWELL VANSTONE

*P*arenting books will tell you different things about how family placement will affect the development of a child's personality. They do not always agree but generally there are similar thoughts on the various family positions and the trend in characteristics. Naturally not every person falls into one of the textbook patterns.

Our third child did not follow any pattern that I had read about, nor was I prepared for the baby I was presented with. Naturally settling in with a newborn is always a learning experience and no two babies will be the same. You always expect some loss of sleep and fatigue, but I had been blessed with two very easy babies previously and thought I had the magic touch with motherhood. God snickered.

Interestingly, the child that gives you the most challenge is the one you spend the most time with and subsequently becomes very close to you. Close in many ways. Like the way you cannot let that child out of your sight and when you cannot see or hear them you are immediately suspicious.

As you know, children grow up and become more independent despite our wish for them to stay little. Our third child went to school at the age of 5 like most Canadian children do. He had loved his life on the farm and never tired of riding with his daddy in the tractor or watching the guys working in the shop. We had no doubt he would become a farmer just like his dad and uncle. At the kindergarten graduation they asked the class ahead of time what they wanted to be when they grew up and the teacher read for each student. There were the typical answers like firefighter, policeman, teacher, and farmer. As she came to our son, we all expected to hear what we knew she would say. "Derek Vanstone wants to be... an astronaut when he grows up." A collective gasp was heard from my family members and then little titters of laughter. Nope, we did not expect that.

Life with Derek was full of unique experiences. Parenting him was so hard during the first 5 years and he did not sleep through the night till after the first year of life and even then, not consistently. I suffered some health issues due to exhaustion. I fully anticipated he would struggle in school. He was the first to publicly testify to his salvation and ask to be baptized. He took his Bible to school for free reading time and set himself apart. He was a rule-follower and enforcer. He was independent in doing his homework and assignments, unlike most children. As Derek got older, he made plans for his future and told us about them with confidence that they would come to be and surprisingly they almost always did.

By grade 12, Derek had been involved in numerous extracurricular activities. He was highly motivated and planned his future in the Air Force. He made appointments for a physical exam and an eye exam and then had interviews and appointments at the recruiting office. We were somewhat oblivious to the serious nature of these things. When he received the call that the Canadian Armed Forces had accepted him to the Officer Training Program, and he would be going to University at the Royal Military College in Kingston, Ontario, it was shocking and yet not. He told us when he was 13 after a trip with cadets that he would be going to school there some day. And so began a career in the military.

Grade 12 was almost over, and Derek informed us that we needed to attend his swearing in ceremony on the 8th of June and that it was very important we be there. A very serious officer made a speech about all the steps these young adults had taken leading up to this moment. He told us about all the forms our children had signed that morning and that even though they were not formally sworn in yet, if they left now and changed their mind about it they would be found and brought back because they now belonged to the Canadian Armed Forces. They did not belong to their mom and dad, but the Forces.

Following this, each person was invited to the front and sworn in, whether on a Bible or not, pledging their allegiance to queen and country. They signed the last form, and it was over. He no longer was just a man, but a soldier.

It was a quiet drive home as we absorbed all that had transpired. The day after grade 12 graduation, Derek flew to Ontario for basic training. We saw him once a year after that for many years and count it a great privilege to call him our son.

7

I AM STRONG

BY MELISSA MONROE

If I had a dollar for every time someone has told me I was strong, I'd have enough money to hunker down and be as weak as I'd like to be for the rest of my life.

I didn't want to be this brand of strong. No one does.

On August 6, 2013, I tried to wake my sweet, two-year-old daughter Alice from her nap. I found her stiff and blue. As a doctor of traditional Chinese medicine, I am professionally trained in CPR, but I was unable to resuscitate her. Paramedics pronounced her dead as I stood under her birthday banner which I'd hung just eleven days prior.

No one knew why Alice died. Aside from a mild cold, she was perfectly healthy. She'd earned a clean bill of health at her doctor's appointment just three days prior. She played for hours before her nap from which she did not awaken. She showed no signs of injury or distress.

There was going to be an autopsy. No one thinks their child will precede them in death, much less require an autopsy. Results could—and did—take months.

Immediately, the coroner suspected Sudden Unexplained Death in Childhood (SUDC), thought it would take months to confirm this. When a child between the ages of one and eighteen dies and a cause of death cannot be determined after a thorough autopsy and death investigation, their death is classified as SUDC. Although rare, it is the 5th leading cause of death in toddlers.

It's a small, shitty club, the membership fees are astronomical, the selection process is a mystery, and absolutely no one wants to join.

Truth be told, I didn't want to live in a world without Alice. I was absolutely paralyzed with guilt. Because we didn't know what happened, I was terrified I'd done – or not done – something that might have contributed to her death. The guilt felt strong enough to kill me. The paramedics, the coroner, my friends, all told me not to feel guilty, that there was nothing I could have done, but my traumatized brain didn't believe them. When there is no clear culprit, we blame ourselves, I suppose. My traumatized brain was trying to annihilate me. But I had to perservere because Grace was still in the world. And Grace – my eldest—was only four-years-old at the time.

How do you live when the pain is so vast it feels like it could kill you? How do you parent when half your heart stopped beating? How do you advise patients when you don't know how your child died and couldn't save her? How do you honor your dead child while nurturing your living child—all while you can barely nurture yourself? How do you provide or experience joy again so your living child doesn't grow up in a macabre mausoleum with a half-alive mother?

I had no idea how to do any of those things, but I knew I had to figure it out. Unfortunately, my mind was mush and not capable of much. Fortunately, I was surrounded by people who supported me while I fumbled through it. I was awestruck at the amount of love directed toward me, encircling me in a seemingly protective shell. My broken heart oozed gratitude at the outpouring of support.

This love, this grace, is what got me out of bed, day after day.

When I didn't know what to do once I was out of bed – which was all day, every day for quite a while—I asked myself, "What would be best for Grace?"

And then I did that, fueled by the immense gratitude I was experiencing.

Lather. Rinse. Repeat.

People kept saying, "I was so strong." Being told you are strong when you feel destroyed is better than a kick in the pants —and it's a gazillion times better than "Be strong!" which is infuriating— but I felt unworthy of the term.

I didn't feel strong whatsoever; I felt shattered. I was experiencing debilitating panic attacks and flashbacks. I couldn't remember anything but the horrific events of August 6th. I had to set alerts on my phone for even the most basic tasks. My body felt like I'd been in a bar fight and slept it off on the concrete in the alley. I cried while I swept the floor. I sobbed when I sorted laundry and realized – again —that Alice's clothes were no longer a part of the wash. I wailed when alone in the car. I felt utterly dismantled, fragile, and the most vulnerable I had ever felt in my life. Being considered "strong" felt like a subpar consolation gift. I didn't want to be strong; I wanted my child to be alive.

But this wasn't a choice I was given, so I tried to train my mind to stop focusing on what I couldn't change and focus on what I could...and continued to use gratitude as my fuel.

Being a parent and a health care professional meant I had many people to care for, regardless of how I felt inside. I was also well aware I was a hot mess and needed to put on my oxygen mask first. So, I made a pledge to do something nurturing for my body/mind/soul for one hour every day. No matter what. Time blocked out in ink in my planner. This self-nurturing was non-negotiable, but it did vary.

Some days I took a hike. Other days, I went to yoga class. Or therapy. Or received body work. Or took a bath. Or swam. Or read something that touched my soul. If something made me feel even the tiniest bit of relief or joy, I added it to the rotation. If something made me feel worse, buh bye.

This was no time to feel worse; I was hanging by a thread.

Every day, I meditated. Every day, I searched out laughter. Every day, I wrote. Every day, I received offers of help—something I wasn't comfortable doing, but even my mush mind knew this was not the time for heroics. Even my battered brain and broken heart knew I could not do this alone. Every day, I sat in stunned silence at the amount of support I received.

Every day, I did what I intuited was best for Grace, and did what felt helpful to me. Then, and only then, did I perform the other tasks of life.

Eventually, after months of writing, my brain felt a little less broken. Eventually, after enough trauma therapy, the panic attacks and flashbacks ceased. Eventually, after enough yoga and massage and swimming and hot baths, my body felt a little less armored. Eventually, after enough comedy clips, my laughter came more freely. Eventually, after enough neighbor's casseroles, I began to cook again. Eventually, I didn't have to block out time to nurture myself; it had become habit.

Eventually, I could think of Alice and smile before the tears fell.

There is no high point to losing a child; it's all downside, believe me. But eventually, doing what would serve Grace led me to serve grace to myself.

Turns out, Grace was perfectly named.

Eventually, I extended enough grace to myself, I realized that being strong does not mean you *feel* strong. Strength is achieved when you feel like you can't, but you do it anyway... without judging yourself too harshly. Strength is achieved when you let people see you at your worst, and let them love you anyway.

And now, by the grace of God, my Grace, and myself, I can say the words, "I am strong" without feeling it's a betrayal of Alice.

8

ON LOSING A CHILD

BY SHEILA WEBSTER

Grief can be so sharp it takes your breath away and you never want to breathe again. Triggers are everywhere, and others don't understand the avenues of the heart, mind and senses that are open.

If you knew them, you would shut all the doorways, windows and crevices through which memory can be triggered. But just as quickly you would run back and reopen them caught in an unending cycle of wanting pain to stop but memories of the loved one to stay intact.

Whether through death or circumstances of life and accumulative effects of living, no pain equals that of losing a child. Movies have been made trying to plumb the depth of a parent's grief and the course of normality, shock, loss, and depression will play in changing their whole world. Nothing, however, touches it.

My great-grandmother solidified this thought in my mind many years ago, as she sat in my parent's living room. Around ninety, stooped in body and spirit, "This is not supposed to happen," she kept saying. "Children are not supposed to die before you." Even though her umpteenth child to have died before her, was my grandmother in her sixties. The order was not right; children should not die first.

Her pain was palpable and unbearable. It wasn't easier at that moment that my grandmother wasn't her little toddler, Rudolph, who was to be buried at sea on the ship from Russia, or my grandmother's twin who was buried on the cold bare prairie near Scapa, dead at thirteen from appendicitis. It was not Danny, her 13-year-old grandson, who had been felled by a bullet from his friend's gun near our home. This was her child, albeit in her sixties, and the pain echoed with all the other losses of her children. Many of her children died before she did. Even though she was a strong German woman who had endured war and its atrocities in her home country, she found the current grief devastating.

My losses of children were not the same as those endured by my great-grandmother, but her body stooped under the weight of grief, gave me some context of historical companionship in my losses. No one follows the same path of grief, and they stumble and falter on the way to healing. No one ever goes back to being the same person they were before the loss.

A person's culture, community, faith, and their family all bring different layers to personal loss and grief and these are to be acknowledged and incorporated along the journey. The more losses the more complicated the path can be.

The loss of a heart-daughter has been one of the hardest to bear. Perhaps, because of the accumulation of losses, her place in my life, her presence, or leave the analyzing off, and maybe *just because I loved her for so long*. The triggers are daily even after six months.

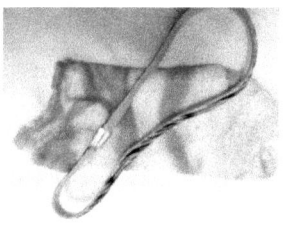

Today it was the sock and hairband. My world is rocked again with her loss. There is no one to talk to, choices were made – losses are irreversible. Crying sometimes helps, but today it only deepens the pain as it courses through the inner channel of other losses.

A hot bath relieves some of the tension; tears mingle with the dead sea salts as the water goes down the drain. I am drained, but somehow closer to her in my memories. I don't know where the other sock went or if there is going to continue to be this infinity of socks who return from the nether world to acknowledge our joint life together.

The sunshine reminds me of her, the rain, driving, night, morning coffee, her school, church, her brothers, flowers, paintings, TV shows, coffee spills, long hair, mischievousness, emptiness. So many things were filled by her in my life.

Spirituality is the only thing that helps me to go on today. Tomorrow I may rail against it, but today it helps.

"You keep track of all my sorrows.

You have collected all my tears in your bottle. (Psalm 56:8, NLT)

Life would become empty if I shut myself off from living and ignored the pain and joy of her memory. My strength will not come from bottling up her loss; it will come in releasing the essence of why I cry.

9

THESE MOMENTS OF MOTHERHOOD

BY SHEILA WEBSTER

There are moments that are joyous in the delivery room, as you wait for your daughter's baby to be born. You calm and soothe her, buy snacks and give encouragement for her partner and pray.

No matter what soul-wrenching and pain they go through, you are just relieved when they hold the little one for the first time. There is no justice in the way they are born —high forceps, caesarean or just a few pushes. No woman births even her own two the same way.

The ticking of the hours with this one was different though. There would be no elation when he was born; he was already deceased. Full term and no explanation. We were both in shock. They wanted her to go home and wait for him to be born, but I didn't believe her mental health could sustain such an added burden.

The hours ticked by in a silent march. We planned his funeral in the deepest dark of the night. You can't help but pray that they are wrong, and he will be alright.

Finally, the last pushes and he was born. For a moment you stubbornly believe he will breathe, But he doesn't. She doesn't want to hold him or see him, and for now that may suffice. Suddenly she asks me to go and make sure he is ok.

The nurse has never done this before either, but we learn together. I hold his little body wrapped in a receiving blanket, blue cap on his head. We clean him carefully. His footprints, and handprints, a little snip of hair.

Discuss his weight, time of birth and record it all. I go back to her and make sure. I tell her as awful as it is there is some comfort and finality to holding him, even just for awhile. He is almost just as perfect as his older brother, and she birthed them both well.

Her body starts healing almost immediately. Awash in the arrangements for the funeral and what he should wear – she doesn't want to exist anymore, and I understand. She has tickets for a concert and asks if it would be wrong to go – I say no it might be therapeutic – she asks me to go with her.

Any other band might not have soothed us the way this one did, but it was healing for moments, and then before it was over, we both had enough and needed to go and cry.

So many decisions made, a perfect little funeral. A few weeks after his little casket was buried, she wished she had held him. I understand, but I remind her she birthed him well and made sure he was not alone.

10

DOES HER HEART BREAK LIKE MINE?

SHEILA MANSELL

Maybe her heart breaks every day like mine, but it is so different. It is always one of choices and she made hers first, I make mine daily.

I think of our child – the one she carried, the one she abandoned that day at court when she didn't show up – she blames me for all of this but I finally stopped believing that somewhere around his half-life ago. Still it was still too long to feel that way for someone who did someone a favour.

Life is complicated enough without taking responsibility for the choices others make beyond our knowing – she made hers – I make mine daily.

He is a gem, but has always had challenges. He was so grey and ashen the first time I saw him—listless, full of fever that didn't show on his cold nine-day-old-six-pound body. I loved babies usually, but him I knew not to attach to at first. He had a very bad case of thrush and was extremely dehydrated. She had sounded so unsure on the phone of what was wrong, insisted she was doing everything right.

Even though she was not my own biological child, I could hear the underlying fear in her voice. "Please mom, come get us – I don't have money for the doctor if he needs something." I mentally weighed the snow falling increasingly outside – the three hour drive one way – my already brimming house of children – the drama she would bring with her – the life of her baby.

"Of course, Abby," I put on my surest mom voice I can muster, "it is not a problem."

Jan 5, there are bills to pay, kids to get ready for school tomorrow, a husband unhappy about being abandoned with the other kids while I pick the troublesome one up. I explain for the millionth time in our marriage – "Tell me Ed – another way to live out my faith – you show me how you can pray for us to make a difference in this world and then be mad at me every time I feel I have to do something. You prayed for her more and that baby when she wasn't taking care of herself, the drugs, and the life on the road – your prayers made a difference."

His eyes were already glazed over and I knew there was no sense. How could one be so surrounded by people of the same faith and feel so alone when they felt a force tugging at them to do the right thing? Urging. Imploring? – How many times had I wished I had no faith so that I could have some peace and ease in the world like so many around me.

Driving was incredibly difficult—the ice on the overpasses, snow snakes writhing across the roads to make drifts. Usually I would have enjoyed a short break from the other mewling and mauling kids I raised, but it was still just the end of the holiday season, hard to leave the warmth of our large, but always in need of repair home.

The storm was so bad I couldn't even enjoy the radio as it took every ounce of concentration to keep the small *Sunfire* on the road – I wished I had borrowed my friend's Saturn, she always had the best winter tires and it had heated seats, satellite radio. I convinced myself that I was coveting a neighbor's property and continued to be thankful at least this was still hugging the scraps of bare pavement it could find between snow and ice.

I thought about my friend Peter – I laughed how funny he could be – how he always told me when I left his and Janine's cozy home after a visit "Keep it between the fences Stella between the fences." The first time he had said that to me I was puzzled until I realized it was another older man's reference to my preference for a bit too much love for the gas pedal. I realized that was a pleasant theme to remember all the older gentlemen that had chided me for the many miles on the road for my calling to broken kids and their evident admiration of what some called spunk and others underlined lovingly as stubbornness and stupidity.

There had been old Herb Norwal, I had accidently passed him once on the highway in our older girl's first car – the *Mercury Mystique*, it had hugged the road nicely, always prowling and asking to rev it up just a little more. Apparently that particular summer day we had been in a hurry to get to a cowboy supper at a nearby small town, I had the main fiddler in the backseat and passed Herb, hoping he was not someone we knew.

Sure enough he recognized Ed in the passenger seat as we passed their car. Later in relating his thoughts on my driving to Ed, he said, "That's what I like, a girl with a little get up and go!" Interesting I thought. At the time I was probably in my mid-thirties but time is funny. Herb had to have been 82 at the time so to him I was almost a newly-minted product, not the middle-aged mom of many I had felt at the time.

As I tried to keep it between the fences, and tried not to lose my patience over the half speed I was able to drive under the conditions I thought about what I was getting myself into. Truthfully I had been into it for years.

I had become Abby's surrogate mom for a while after finding her starving on the streets of our small city. Her slight, shivering frame, over five years ago, was cold on a December evening. There were skinny jeans slagging off her wisp of a barely teen body, strawberry hair hanging in frozen shards around her freckled and made up face, sneakers with no socks, and an oversized man's hoodie to complete her ensemble. 25 below zero and so cold it took almost two days, a gallon of chicken soup, another of hot chocolate, numerous baths, blankets and grilled cheese to warm her core.

I started to laugh. Another generation born to the same family line and now here it was 32 below zero and a blizzard, travelling to find the offspring of that young teen, another in need of mothering. I finally arrived at the house and tempered my anger, her boyfriend Mack, some of his family members with their progeny all around.

Inside my head I screamed, "How could there be all these adults around this baby and he is so sick and they don't know what to do?" I brought myself into check for the drama I sensed would begin. As if on cue from stage right Abby threw herself at Mack, and streamed large lines of mascara via her sobbing down his confused young face and dark t-shirt.

"I can't leave you Mack, I don't know what to do – but our baby – our baby is so sick." It was her very true and real life, but she should have received an Oscar at some moments of it. It was clear to my mother's eye that she wanted to leave yesterday, but had waited because she wanted to be stable.

"It's ok Abby; you will be back in a couple days. We'll just take little Garret to the doctor in the city and be back in no time," I tried to soothe our way out the door as the weather was not getting better or the night any earlier.

Mack looked a mixture of panic, relief, and resentment. He barely knew me. I honestly think he hardly knew Abby. Mack's sister Gerda started to get in my face, "I don't know why you think you can do anything different for Garret – I have raised these three and they are fine. Abby is just being dramatic." I looked down at the six pound bundle that should have been close to his birth weight of over seven pounds, his pallid appearance. Abby could be dramatic I thought, but she had understated the baby's condition. I wondered if he would make it two hours to the doctor, let alone be ok.

"Ok Gerda, I am sure Abby is no different than you were when you had your first baby. She probably just needs some mom time with me, some rest and pampering. No need for accusation from any of us. I know you have taken the best care you could of all of them." I looked down at her assortment of dirty and whiny cherubs pulling at her skirt with overfilled diapers.

I knew I was being as diplomatic with my words as I could, under the circumstances. There were lots of adult entertainment items in the home, carefully carved out places to play games and such. There were open food boxes, but little nutrition or nurturing evident, throughout the messy albeit newer than mine, bungalow. It had just been Christmas ten days ago, but nothing was picked up for the event, and it was intermingled with dishes caked with macaroni and cheese scraps, old toast pieces, and...I stopped trying to categorize other visible items.

"When did he last eat?" I asked no one in particular. Gerda answered first, "I tried to give him apple juice a couple hours ago but he wouldn't take it, so I figured he would learn to eat when he was hungry like mine did. You can't spoil them too much."

Abby knew me well enough to see my minor signs of irritations not being hidden behind my pasted on patient smile, "Mom, I tried to breast feed him about three this afternoon, but he wouldn't suck."

Oh Good Lord! I thought as I looked at the clock and it was nine pm. Probably at least a good eight hours without hydration! Maybe for the first time I felt like my gut feeling was right, and that Ed's frustration with this particular mission was misplaced. There was no way if he felt Garret was this sick that he would have made a fuss. He hated to see babies and small children hurt.

I picked up the weightless car seat and its cargo, while pulling Abby firmly off Mack with the other arm. "Mack can you bring the bag to the car, and finish your goodbyes out there? The roads are bad and I am sure you want us to be as safe as possible." Mack sprang into action as he finally had something that made sense to do. A playpen, and several bags came with it and I wondered what her real plan was and how I could get it all in the car.

Finally on the road, I let Abby talk non-stop; it was the only way to get as much of the real story out of her as possible. No editing on my part, just non-stop grandiose storytelling. I was able to discern a fairly normal birth, jaundice under lights for two days, no troubles with breastfeeding in the hospital. I became even more horrified at his condition though when I realized he really had only been home five days. She had been drinking lots of fluids, coffee and pop mostly I assumed from the assortment of bottles and cups on the counter I had seen.

By the time we got to emergency care I had enough of the info to get in. I knew there would be no insurance or health card, no ID. I had had to do this for so many kids I knew the drill. Seem repentant, tell them you would get back to them in the morning with the correct information, let them photocopy as much of my ID as would satisfy them, promise them the moon in exchange for a quick look from the doctor or nurse practitioner to confirm my mom diagnosis. It was always about the paper trail when you were dealing with things like this.

Because he was so young they actually put us in fairly quickly which was a relief. I knew it would be a quick IV to rehydrate and a prescription. I had stopped at the drugstore and got most of what I knew they would tell me to get after I went, because I knew it would be closed by the time we got out of emergency and he was in need of stuff.

He had a bad case of thrush and the nurse pulled me aside on the way out to let me know that it was because the mom was not cleaning her nipples off. He meant on her body, not the bottle, but probably them as well. He insisted he had seen this in other girls and despite the fact that she evidently loved her baby; he said it would be best to teach her how to sterilize bottles and formula feed the baby.

I hated the idea but in this case my gut told me he was right. In my calculations I had figured it would cost for the baby`s prescriptions, forgotten diapers etc., but had neglected to think about what she might have that needed tending to – drugstore stuff and prescriptions were over $200 that we didn't have, and that hadn't included the gas. This city was still almost two hours of driving in the swirling snowstorm to get to our small one. Thankfully Ed and the kids would all be asleep when I returned, so no questions till morning and there were too many kids to make questions worthwhile anyway while making breakfast.

Garret perked up over the next few days and I could see he was a bright little guy. He just needed a chance, a chance his mom wouldn't know how to give him. I was determined not to get attached which was hard as I adored babies.

Abby and I fought about breastfeeding and a hundred other things over the next nine days. She loved the mothering I gave her, but was strong-willed as she needed to be for her life on and off the streets – in and out of average living. I knew she still trusted me though and tried to make things as easy as possible on her. No matter what her temperament or how she treated us, she was still a good girl deep down and a new mom trying to make it.

Four weeks after I returned a healthier Abby and Garret to Mack, she phoned me in the height of hysteria. He had been apprehended by social services, she wanted me to get him. Once again, Ed and I fought about what our place is in the world—who are the widows and orphans of today, and that we can't save everyone. I totally agreed, but knew I would bear the brunt from everyone about this but chose to do what my gut said I needed to – be there for a helpless baby and try and get his mom on her feet.

Eighteen months flew by. Abby couch-surfed and lived on and off with some family when they weren't fighting in the same city. Life had taken an easy rhythm with my two favourite times of the day with Garret being in the morning when he would wake in my room before everyone else, and at night when his cousin Lee who I had acquired sometime after I met Abby would sit on the couch for Garret's last bottle of the day. Lee would discuss with me how his family felt about me having Garret and what he felt would be best for him. Lee was determined I needed to keep him.

I steadfastly chose to believe Abby would come around. Abby and I attended parenting classes together, she had gone for oodles of counselling, "She will come around," I patiently told him. I honoured Garret's Metis heritage by not cutting his hair until the day he was returned to his mother if she chose to cut it then.

Abby's visits became erratic, Mack came occasionally. She started bringing other guys around trying out different daddy combinations thinking that would somehow circumvent the issues she refused to face in her own life. She had her day in court which I begged her not to do and just stick with the counselling and direction her social worker was giving her. But I think Abby thought court was some shortcut through the hard stuff.

They awarded me permanent guardianship the day she didn't come back for court. I had left her at the crossroads, against my will a week earlier.

We had run to town to see our separate lawyers and Garret's social worker the week before the final verdict in court. It was always such a surreal scene—she was wanting custody of Garret, but not willing to finish her conditions. She knew if she could put on a good show in court she would win. But she had no other ride. We could combine a visit and have some 'mother-daughter' time as well. She revealed her real plan to me just after she had assured the social worker she would not leave and would go through with court. In between hot McDonald's fries, which were always a staple of these trips, she assured me she knew what she was doing and not to worry.

Garret was cooing in the backseat with a ball and a truck, when she kissed him. She had me pull over at the gas station on the corner of two highways. She had a ruddy complexion and had kept some of her baby fat from pregnancy, so it hung over her skinny jeans that were fairly full, her hair was straight and clean, shining like spun silk, reflecting gold and strawberry as the spring late-morning eastern sun hit it. She had a small backpack with supplies, maybe an extra change of clothes. She needed to get away for a week she said, going to find Mack a province or two away. She was going to scratch his eyes out for abandoning her and the baby with her best friend the '*ho*'.

"You know you would do it Mom. I'll be back. I can't leave my baby, you know that."

It was only then I knew she wasn't coming back; I almost panicked at something I had held at bay. At over forty I would now be

Garret's mom, permanently. I understood her better than anyone had in her life but I had hid the truth from myself since the night I picked his listless little body up at nine days old.

You can't stop destiny, once you choose to pick up the phone. You can't change who you are at your core – it is easier for a leopard to change its spots. I became Garrett's mom, not the day the government awarded him to me in a family court. I became his mom on a snowy January evening when I couldn't turn my back on another human being. A wisp of a girl in leftover clothes, who broke her mom's and son's hearts, but whose heart breaks like mine.

THE STRENGTHS OF MY MOTHER

BY SHEILA AMY MANSELL (THIRD IN THE LINE OF FOUR GENERATIONS OF WRITERS)

*E*ven though my mother spent more of her life doing other things, I think of her most, and she is happiest when she is reading or writing. She has always longed to be closer to us children, but in a way is more comfortable with the writing on the pages, whether it came from her pen, computer, or was printed in a book or magazine.

In my mind, my mother is suspended in age somewhere between twenty-five and fifty. She was twenty five when she gave birth to me, the second of her children and first daughter, and fifty when I became a mother.

The first memory I have of her as my mother is of watching her in the kitchen perhaps of our small one-bedroom home.

Memories are fleeting, as soon as you begin to peer at one sometimes the flicker reel is already somewhere else, and only seems to stop on those things we remembered most often.

To me often my relationship with my mother is a little more voyeuristic than tangible. She related to me once that when I was a baby, she couldn't nurture me perhaps in the way she wanted to, often leaving me for hours to lie in my crib. After some time, I stopped crying for her, she was busy. Her recollections of me thereafter always appear that I am just out of her reach and not quite understandable.

For her life was a puzzle of, 'How did we get to this stage already?' She was always somewhere back in time or forward in the future, never quite present but always trying.

I would watch her, as she answered the black cradle telephone of the east side of the rose and mint papered kitchen wall, beside the row of white framed kitchen windows. Sometimes happy for its intrusions, other times frustrated trying to figure out how to appease whoever was on the mysterious other end of the phone.

There were not many places to go in our house, the crib to see my sister, follow my brother and our dog outside if we were allowed.

In the early days, I don't think she read as much, three babies in quick succession, a budding heating business, company using our white screen door like a revolving one. My grandmother and some of her children lived across someone else's garden plot – so there was a lot of comedy and drama to watch with their interactions.

My father's mother at times could be very sharp in her German way – muttering things I could not understand. At a young age I vowed I would learn her secret language to know what she was really saying to my mother or us, and I did in high school.

Looking back, I wonder now how deeply my mother could be affected by some of the things that happened across the garden with not much else but so many things that needed tending.

Washing day in the winter was such fun for us children – large frozen sheets brought in from the line for us to bravely crawl through before they collapsed. In response to this my father made a wooden cage (I call it a cage because we used to imagine it was an old lion box!) taller than we were and longer with dowels across it and holes in the end. My mother would hang the winter wash in this and the fan he got would blow air in. It was never clear to me if she thought it worked or was more work.

Dad always seemed to be trying to invent or do things to make her life a little easier. Perhaps he didn't understand all the stress she felt with us children, the business, her in-laws, but from my silent movie of their life I see how his actions were always striving toward making a better life for her. She maybe longed for more words, but he spoke volumes in actions.

From her earliest beginnings her life was surrounded by losses, which maybe made the comfort and stability of books more appealing.

Her uncle Donald, Able Bodied Seaman William Donald McCrindle, had been the light of her life as a small child. His stability, charm and strength, was the glue that held life as she knew it together. When he died in action in 1944, his warmth, youth and memory brought her solace during times of loneliness, and the sheer struggle of her family to survive in Northern Saskatchewan.

Her grandmother and aunts ran a home for the aged, and their loss was abundant and life often scary for a youngster. Her three siblings, all boys, were added in quick succession – forcing her to become the older sibling at a time perhaps when she needed comfort and security.

She revealed once that her father was often frustrated with her 'daydreaming' to the point that one day when she was 12, he took her favourite toy and only doll and chopped it up with an axe in retaliation for her reading and once again leaving chores undone.

I learned of this strange act, when my grandfather came down our lane with a large Wendy walker type doll. It seemed strange that he should arrive with such a doll on a summer day. It was no one's birthday. Moments later life became even stranger as he wordlessly handed it to my mother. It was not for one of us three young girls, but for a full-grown married woman, my mother, my grandfather's grown daughter. My mother burst into tears. It was not until years later that she divulged the reason for the gift from her father.

Living in a world of boys, she also found the normality of being a girl, was odd to them, and made her feel like an outsider perhaps. They grew up for some time in a one room cabin – no privacy for anyone, but especially excruciating for a girl of twelve.

Summer was a longed-for season in her life. She could lie in the fields reading a book, thunder across a field on a horse, or generally just have some privacy for her thoughts and self.

Pictures of my mother from that time show a shy wallflower of a girl against the backdrop of poverty. Anne-Shirley-like with pigtails and an uncertain smile.

Her life is fragmented to me – a story was told to me by her uncle a short time before his death. The gentleman had been a hobby paleontologist with stacks of rocks, bones and other artifacts in his home. He was my grandpa's sister's husband, not a relative by blood, so to speak.

His objective opinion of my grandfather was not the most complimentary when it came to grandpa providing for his family. "His mother and a couple of sisters took the long train ride from Drumheller one year, to northern Saskatchewan to see how the growing family was fairing. Nothing could have prepared them for the shocking reality of the conditions my brothers-in-law family was enduring." he recollected, from the shadows of his over-stuffed living room.

"Things your mother must have had to endure," he went on, "Well my mother-in-law was horrified. There were broken bits of furniture strewn in the yard, broken down farming implements, dirty children and no food to be seen." He related to me upon their arrival back home in Alberta, my grandfather's family, comfortable, though not well to do, gathered supplies and food and farm tools and loaded them in a box car to send for their survival.

Stories of my mother's growing up years were few and far between, much of it she was uncertain anyone would find interesting. Some of it she was ashamed they had endured.

Whatever happened up north, the family of six finally migrated en masse back to regions close to his family in the Drumheller/Rosebud area.

My mother met my father in Drumheller where she had been working at a store as a clerk. She was nineteen, he twenty-one. One of them for sure was smitten at first sight. Their dating and engagement were typical of that time, with the exception perhaps that my father already was helping raise a large family, his siblings.

Both had dreams of a better life. They would build a better life than the one they had been handed by their forefather's choices and the hand life had dealt them. Despite what they felt at many junctures over the years, they did succeed at this. My mother and father never allowed life to sink to the level of desperate survival and deprivation both of them had grown up with.

Life must have been frustrating for my mother at many times over the years we were growing up. She had had dreams of her own, but circumstance and need dictated a portion of her life she had not been prepared for. Marriage to her had meant freedom to some degree—freedom from the shackles of life in her family. As much as she loved them, she wanted choices and a career.

My father was young, strong, a hard worker, good provider and probably had a thousand unrealized dreams of his own. Having a life partner to take care of some of the other details of his life, and such a good looking one who seemed full of spunk and spark probably seemed like a dream come true.

They moved around a bit. A trailer in Vermillion, AB where my brother was born. A rented house with poor heating, where chicks were raised on the second floor. In one of these places my mother said that my brother's bottle was often frozen in the early mornings of winter.

Finally, a home was obtained in Red Deer, a small one-bedroom with outdoor toilet. But it was stability for almost 20 years before they were forced by the city to build a new home, because the city had developed the once farmland around them to be a new subdivision. They have lived in that new house now for about 40 years and almost 60 within that same parcel of land.

I remember my mom's excitement over choosing the colours of their home, curtains, furniture – it was tempered by practicalities but there remains one lacy curtain, and one floral that was closer to her dreams.

She made 1000s of meals and entertained 1000s of guests in that home. She has handwritten 1000s of encouragement cards, emails and other letters from that home.

The petunias in front of the home, annually planted are kind of a homage to her father. Other flowers around the house are a mix of what reminds us of my father's family and hers, and a bit of their own preferences.

In that home she launched the four of us children, welcomed grandchildren and now great-grandchildren. Still, she feels somewhat on the fringes of life most days. Once she was a journalist.

My grandfather had wanted to take a journalism course when he was a young man. His father however told him to put the foolishness away, and he did put the course in a trunk and entered an unsuccessful life of working for a living at things he did not want to do. His writing life reappeared and blossomed upon his retirement almost fifty years later, when he penned almost 1000 poems before his death.

My mother for a time, was a local news correspondent in our prairie city. That was until it began to interfere with her role as our mother. The unthinkable happened one day as she missed her bus home, while out on assignment and toting my youngest sister with her. She arrived home to find my next-in-line sister had come home to an empty house.

My mother, like her father, put away her dreams of being a budding newspaper person, and put her efforts to the task at hand of raising a young family, growing a business and tending the mother-in-law and various other duties of the early seventies.

Oddly enough my grandfather, my mother and later I lived parallel lives in different times without trying. For sometime, I worked for a newspaper as a sports editor but hated it, because of the angle I had to put on every piece I observed and wrote. I didn't mind the various columns for other newspapers I wrote over the years, but it was not a dream I had wanted to achieve. A daughter of mine has been interviewed at times, another girl I raised writes for a local paper as well. Without realizing it at times we follow in the footsteps of those before us.

My mother still sees herself as weak and others as well. But those of us who know her best and understand trapped trauma, no matter how conflicted at times, know that she is one of the stronger people we know.

She hosts even those who do not agree with her with as much grace and flair as an over-eighty barely-sighted person can.

My mother follows all her grandchildren, nieces and nephews and greats as closely as she can, and she always prays for everyone.

She dreamed of being a writer, an author, maybe an artist and traveller. Maybe it has not been exactly what she dreamed but she has always lived way beyond the walls of her home and been interested in the wider world and galaxies beyond.

www.ingramcontent.com/pod-product-compliance
Lightning Source LLC
Chambersburg PA
CBHW071400080526
44587CB00017B/3146